Scribbles, Stickers & Glue

A Kids' Guide to Scrapbooking

Scribbles, Stickers & Glue
A Kids' Guide to Scrapbooking

Nikki Larsen

Sterling Publishing Co., Inc. New York
A Sterling/Chapelle Book

Chapelle, Ltd.: Jo Packham, Sara Toliver, Cindy Stoeckl

Editors: Ray Cornia and Jennifer Luman
Art Director: Karla Haberstich
Graphic Illustrator: Kim Taylor
Copy Editor: Marilyn Goff
Staff: Kelly Ashkettle, Areta Bingham, Anne Bruns, Donna Chambers,
    Emily Frandsen, Lana Hall, Susan Jorgensen, Melissa Maynard, Barbara
    Milburn, Lecia Monsen, Suzy Skadburg, Kim Taylor, Desirée Wybrow

If you have any questions or comments, please contact:
  Chapelle, Ltd., Inc., P.O. Box 9252, Ogden, UT 84409
  (801) 621-2777 · (801) 621-2788 Fax
  e-mail: chapelle@chapelleltd.com
  web site: www.chapelleltd.com

Library of Congress Cataloging-in-Publication Data
Larsen, Nikki.
Scribbles, stickers & glue : a kids' guide to scrapbooking / Nikki Larsen.
p. cm.
"A Sterling/Chapelle Book."
Includes index.
ISBN 1-4027-0920-X
1. Photographs—Conservation and restoration—Juvenile literature. 2.
Photograph albums—Juvenile literature. 3. Scrapbooks—Juvenile litera-
ture. I. Title: Scribbles, stickers and glue. II.. Title.
TR465.L36 2004
745.593—dc22
                         2004000941

10 9 8 7 6 5 4 3 2 1

Published in paperback in 2005 by Sterling Publishing Co., Inc.
387 Park Avenue South, New York, NY 10016
© 2004 by Nikki Larsen
Distributed in Canada by Sterling Publishing
% Canadian Manda Group, 165 Dufferin Street,
Toronto, Ontario, Canada M6K 3H6
Distributed in Great Britain & Europe by Chris Lloyd at Orca Book Services,
Stanley House, Fleets Lane, Poole BH15 3AJ England
Distributed in Australia by Capricorn Link (Australia) Pty. Ltd.
P. O. Box 704, Windsor, NSW 2756, Australia

Printed and Bound in China
All Rights Reserved

Sterling ISBN 1-4027-0920-X Hardcover
        ISBN 1-4027-2785-2 Paperback

For information about custom editions, special sales, premium and
corporate purchases, please contact Sterling Special Sales
Department at 800-805-5489 or specialsales@sterlingpub.com.

The Lemonade Stand

There was a nice lady who had
a plan.

The kids in the neighborhood
would make up her clan.

We will save the animals in this
land.

To do it, let's make a Lemonade
Stand.

We'll sell drinks, candy,
necklaces, and much more.

And soon customers will be
knocking at our door.

The Animal Sanctuary will get
the money we make.

Because, don't all animals
deserve a break?

Introduction

Hey Kids!

OK! So you want to do some scrapbooking. It is really quite easy. The most important thing is to have fun, be silly, and show everyone who you are and what you do. *Scribbles, Stickers & Glue: A Kids' Guide to Scrapbooking* shows you fun techniques such as how to transform your everyday Halloween photographs into a spooky encounter, using a simple method called Glue Line and Tin Foil Relief. Sound hard? It is simple to do.

Have you ever wanted to play with shaving cream? Well, now you can make fabulous papers while you are doing it. Has your Mom ever asked you not to blow bubbles in your milk with a straw? Now it is a requirement if you want to make Bubble Prints.

Message to Parents

Although this book is about children being creative on their own, it is also an excellent opportunity for you to show support, guidance, and encouragement. This interaction may take place while selecting papers or craft supplies for a specific page layout, as a sounding board for bouncing off ideas, or most importantly, the acknowledgment and excitement in the final product. Kids thrive and respond to all positive reinforcement and through this, their creativity and artistic ability will soar. Creativity sparks innovation in all areas, not solely exclusive to art, music, and dance, but engineering, mathematics, research, and politics. It opens the mind to search and grasp for new solutions in every aspect of our daily lives.

These scrapbooking ideas will not only capture a moment in time, but will reflect your child's artistic expressions. *Scribbles, Stickers & Glue: A Kids' Guide to Scrapbooking* has listed projects into general age ranges, but with a little help from an adult, they are appropriate for children of any age.

Creativity in art is a way for kids to act out their thoughts, emotions, and personalities. The way we, as parents, interact and encourage them will help to increase their confidence, pride, satisfaction, and respect.

Beyond the magic your children will create in their scrapbook projects, they will be secure in their heart, realizing that you respect their thoughts and enjoy their company—a requirement our kids deserve.

So pull up a chair, get out the photographs, and let's start making scrapbook pages. It is fun, it is easy, and it is something both children and adults will enjoy.

Nikki

Table of Contents

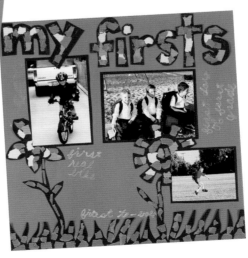

General Information

To the Parent:

Scrapbooking is a popular activity all across the country. It can also be expensive. In creating this book for children, the purpose was two-fold. Firstly, activities were developed for children that would be fun, educational, simple, and involved family participation. Materials were selected that were inexpensive yet resulted in interesting elements for a scrapbook page.

Secondly, the activities show some scrapbook pages that are more appropriate for individual display than for assembling in a book. Oftentimes, young scrapbookers cannot wait to display their work. In these cases, a display item is more rewarding for the child than a neatly assembled scrapbook. In participating in these activities, the child will capture more of themselves than just their image on a photograph.

Creative Tool Kit

Often, adults who enjoy scrapbooking have a collection of tools and materials to use when making their scrapbook pages, kids should too. Below, you'll find a shopping list of some of the basic tools and materials needed to complete the projects in this book and the best places to purchase them.

Scrapbook or Craft Store
Alphabet stickers
Card stocks
Decals
Die-cuts
Glue sticks
Papers
Permanent colored markers
Photo corners
Photo tape
Stickers

Art Supply or University Book Store
Book bone
Oil pastels
Pastels
Squeegee
Watercolor paper

Craft Store

Acrylic paints
Black graphite transfer paper
Chalks
Cutting surface
Spray mounting adhesive
Paintbrushes
Ribbons
Thin-gauge wire
Utility knife

Home Improvement Center

Large metal ruler
Spray paints

Grocery Store

Colored pencils
Crayons
Fruits and veggies for making prints
Pencils
School glue
Scissors
Shaving cream
Shoe polish
Styrofoam trays
Tin foil

For the more advanced crafter, try using advanced tools and materials such as those listed below. Substitute these products for the basic materials used in the projects to get more decorative effects.

Advanced Tools

Circle cutter
Decorative-edged scissors
Linoleum gouges
Paper punches
Rotary paper cutter
Templates

Advanced Materials

Acid-free glues
Acid-free papers
Acid-free paper covers
Background papers
Rubber cement

Helpful Hints & Learning Tips

• Always save scraps. Scrap paper is great to have on hand when a scrapbook page needs an extra touch.

• When making printed paper, don't forget to make a couple of extras. It may be just what another page needs or simply perfect for a homemade card.

• If one of the techniques does not produce the perfect effect, start over and save the paper. Use the back side to border photographs, or it may come in handy for a different project later.

• Always write the date on each page. If the page is simple, without any narration, use a pencil and write the date in small numbers on the front or back of the page.

Photography Ideas

• Color and texture help add interest in photography. Pay particular attention to different shapes and colors of objects such as leaves, rocks, and flowers.

• The best pictures seem to be taken when the person is not aware a picture is being taken. They tend to be more relaxed and natural.

• When shooting with a film camera, use the best possible camera for the circumstances. Naturally, if the child is too young to handle an expensive camera, a disposable camera works great in this situation and is durable enough for kids to use.

Throughout the Book

• Throughout the book you and your children will learn techniques, followed by 3–5 projects that use each technique. After learning the techniques, put your imagination work to come up with creative ways to use that technique to create your own project.

• These scrapbooking ideas will not only capture a moment in time, but will reflect your child's dreams, goals, and desires as well as creative and artistic expressions at that age.

• Throughout the book you will find hints for making the technique or project easier, faster, or more practical. You will also find *Words to Know* that will help children understand some of the terms used in the instructions. It just may be possible to learn a little something along the road to having fun. Wouldn't that be great!

• By the way, your first two *Words to Know* are listed below.

 Words to Know

Corresponding means to be in harmony or compatible. So, if your layout page has blue, red, and yellow dots, corresponding paper colors would be blue, red, and yellow.

Narrate means to tell a little about the photographs on a layout page. Use alphabet stickers, crayons, markers, or pencils to narrate.

Getting Down & Dirty

Now, let the fun begin! Roll up your sleeves because it is time to get your hands dirty, make messes, create wonderful art, take hilarious photographs of your friends. Let the scrapbooking party begin!

Shaving Cream & Paint Paper

TECHNIQUE

This is a great project for young children. They will be able to play in shaving cream while creating a gorgeous piece of paper to use on any scrapbook page.

Hint: Do this project close to a sink. It makes rinsing the paper much easier.

Technique Tools & Materials

Acrylic paints
Card stock
Cookie sheet
Pencil or toothpick
Shaving cream

Instructions

1. Place enough shaving cream into the bottom of cookie sheet to cover an area approximately 1" deep.

2. Squeeze a thin line of each color of acrylic paint across the shaving cream.

3. Using a pencil or toothpick, make wavy lines or circles into the paint.

4. Lay card stock on top of the shaving cream and press down. Make certain all areas of card stock are pressed firmly into shaving cream.

5. Place paper under warm, running water to remove excess paint and shaving cream. Lay paper on a flat surface to dry.

P R O J E C T

Swimming Party

Project Tools & Materials

Card stocks: black, dark blue, light blue, white

Glue stick

Markers

Photographs

Scissors

Instructions

1. Follow the instructions for **Shaving Cream & Paint Paper** on page 12 using blue, black, and white paint on blue paper.

2. Let paper dry thoroughly and begin decorating process.

3. Using a pencil, sketch water drops in several different sizes onto each color of card stock and cut them out.

4. Glue the photographs onto the black card stock and glue the water drops coming off the corners of the photographs.

5. Carefully cut out around each photograph and the splashing water drops.

6. Glue them onto the shaving cream paper and using a marker, narrate the page.

THAT'S A HEAD OF HAIR!

PROJECT

THAT'S A HEAD OF HAIR!

Safety Note: Never place supporting hand in front of utility knife. Adults will need to supervise this activity.

Project Tools & Materials

8" x 10" Photograph

Blue card stock

Glue stick

Scissors

Transfer paper

Utility knife

White marker

Instructions

1. Follow instructions 1–3 for **Shaving Cream & Paint Paper** on page 12.

2. Swirl the first color of paint across the shaving cream. Turn the cookie sheet one quarter turn, then add the second color. Turn the cookie sheet another quarter turn, add the third color. Make another quarter turn and add fourth color.

3. Using a toothpick or pencil, make small swirls into the shaving cream and paint. This will resemble a curly head of hair.

4. Follow instructions 4–5 for **Shaving Cream & Paint Paper**.

5. Once the paper has dried, lay transfer paper with graphite side down on top of shaving cream paper.

6. Place photograph on top of transfer paper. Using a pencil, trace around hairline, over shoulders, down chest, and come to point at bottom of photograph.

7. Remove photograph and transfer paper. Using a utility knife, make a small X in the center of transfer paper marks.

8. Using scissors, cut out around transfer paper marks.

Hint: Always cut on the inside of the marks and cut more away as you need to. Remember, you can always cut more away, but once it has been cut, you can not bring it back.

9. Glue photograph and shaving cream and paint paper onto the page. Using a white marker, narrate the page.

PROJECT

My Best Work

• Things other than photographs can be scrapbooked. This technique is a great way to show off exceptional schoolwork.

• To make this page, follow the instructions for making **Shaving Cream & Paint Paper** on page 12. Use silver paint with black and red in your shaving cream and a black card stock border behind your work.

• Another important lesson for scrapbookers is to use different types of borders. Some items such as this spelling paper work very well with straight, square borders.

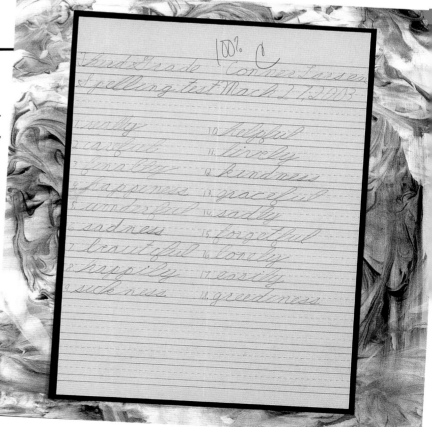

Thats My Grammy

My big brother
and me

1 MONTHOLD   2000

1 Day Old   2000

He's the best

1 year old   2001

P R O J E C T

When I Was Little

• To re-create this page, make **Shaving Cream & Paint Paper** using the instructions on page 12. Then use the paper as a background for the photographs.

• Use colors in your shaving cream that coordinate with the colors in your photographs.

• To make the page more colorful and interesting, add borders behind your photographs and premade paper flowers as accents on the page.

P R O J E C T

JUST ME & GRAMPS

• Follow the instructions for **Shaving Cream & Paint Paper** on page 12. Instead of using the paper as a background for your photographs, here the photograph is set off from this busy background by a scrap paper border.

• To make this page, use a large border in a color that coordinates with the paint and photograph.

Linoleum Block Images

TECHNIQUE

Safety Note: Never place supporting hand in front of gouge. Adults will need to supervise this activity.

 Words to Know

A **brayer** is a rubber roller used to apply the ink to printing surfaces.

The word **lino** is short for linoleum.

Technique Tools & Materials

2" x 5½" Soft-linoleum printing block
Black ink
Card stock or paper to print onto
Marker
Plastic dinner plate
Rubber brayer
Set of linoleum-cutting gouges
Soft-lead pencil

Instructions

1. Using a soft-lead pencil, sketch image onto lino block.

   Hint: All images will be reversed from original drawing when printed. Also, the image you wish to appear on paper is the one *not* carved out of the lino.

2. Using a marker, color-in any areas of lino surface *not* to be gouged out.

3. Begin by using the largest V-shaped gouge for making initial outline cuts. This will quickly eliminate large areas you do not want to print. Use smaller-sized gouges for intricate areas.

4. Follow contour of image by using directional gouges. Remember to not cut too deeply. Ridge patterns may create beautiful textures.

5. Once gouging out linoleum is completed, squeeze penny-sized dot of ink onto plastic plate.

6. Using a brayer, roll out ink into a crisscross pattern until ink is smooth and begins to feel slightly sticky. Roll the brayer across the lino.

7. Place lino image face down onto card stock and press firmly on all sides and corners. Press fingers firmly over the entire back surface of the printing block. Secure card stock and remove lino block so image will not smear.

P R O J E C T

My Sadie Dog

Project Tools & Materials

Card stock
Glue stick
Patterned paper
Photograph
Stickers: alphabet, numbers

Instructions

1. Sketch drawings of your pet onto lino and follow instructions for making **Linoleum Block Images** on page 18 and above.

2. Print lino onto lower half of patterned paper.

3. Glue photograph above lino print and mount patterned paper onto card stock.

4. Using alphabet and number stickers, tell a little about your pet.

PROJECT

Apple of My Eye

Project Tools & Materials

Apple-patterned tissue paper
Black marker
Card stocks: light green, red, yellow
Eye pattern
Glue stick
Paintbrush
Photographs
School glue
Scissors
Transfer paper

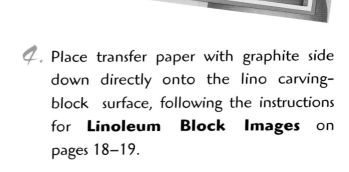

Instructions

1. To make the layout page, cut out several apple images from the tissue paper. Use images that run off the tissue paper edge. These images will give a natural edge for paper and less cutting will be required.

2. Dilute school glue slightly. Using a paintbrush, paint glue onto an area of light-green card stock. Place tissue paper on top of wet glue. Brush over image lightly again with diluted glue.

3. Continue adding apple images onto layout page. Let design dry thoroughly.

4. Place transfer paper with graphite side down directly onto the lino carving-block surface, following the instructions for **Linoleum Block Images** on pages 18–19.

5. Lay the pattern of the eye on top of transfer paper.

6. Trace over the pattern with pencil or pen. The image will transfer directly onto lino.

7. Using a gouge, carve around eye image and carve small apple in eye center.

8. Print apple of my eye image onto layout page, making certain image overlaps some of apple tissue paper.

9. While the ink is drying, crop and border your photographs with yellow card stock followed by red card stock.

10. Glue photographs in place.

11. Using a black marker, narrate with the words: *apple of my eye.*

In the Garden

This project provides a great opportunity for parents to introduce art to babies and toddlers.

IN THE GARDEN
Summer 2001

- Follow the instructions for **Linoleum Block Images** on pages 18–19. Using a pencil, encourage your baby or toddler to scribble and draw over entire carving-block lino. Carefully cut around each scribble. Notice that some of the sketches are thicker while some are very thin.

- Cut around sketches to create linear variety. Finish by stamping the lino onto the pages and adding photographs.

PROJECT

A Star, an Angel & a Dove

• Follow the instructions for making **Lino-leum Block Images** on pages 18–19. On these pages a star, an angel, and a dove are carved into the lino to create a holiday page.

• You may want to use the lino after making this page for creating homemade holiday cards to send to your friends and family.

• On this side of your two-page spread, stamp the lino all over the page, then border the photographs with holiday paper.

• You can use different background papers on each page. Using the same lino will tie the pages together.

Object Prints

Ages 3 and up

This is another great technique to use with young children and toddlers. It will reinforce learning their shapes and colors.

Try using objects such as fruits and vegetables cut in half, juice glasses, leaves, lipstick lids, buttons, corks, sponges, forks, toothbrushes, potato masher, slotted spoon, and cereal.

Hints: Make certain to leave some areas on the background paper showing, being careful so the prints do not overpower other parts of your scrapbook page design. This will help tie your page together.

• Have a piece of newspaper handy to lay your objects on once you have paint on them.

• If you use household items to make your prints, be certain that you wash them well to remove all of the paint.

Technique Tools & Materials
Acrylic paints (3 colors)
Card stock
Objects for printing
Paper plate
Photographs

Instructions

1. Squeeze paints onto paper plate so colors touch one another.

2. One by one, place objects into paint, then stamp onto card stock.

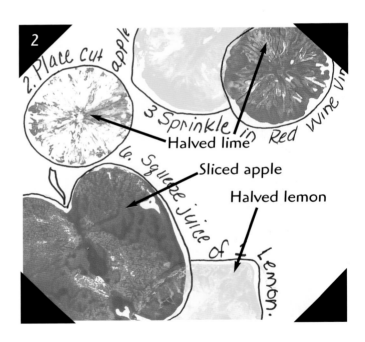

Halved lime
Sliced apple
Halved lemon

3. Continue until the page is covered with prints as desired.

4. Crop and border photographs and glue them onto the page.

P R O J E C T

SOUR APPLES

Project Tools & Materials

- Apple treat recipe
- Card stock
- Fruits: apple, lemon, lime
- Marker
- Pencil
- Red scrap paper
- Utility knife

Instructions

1. Crop (if needed) and border a photograph of your favorite apple treat with red scrap paper.

2. Place the photograph onto the piece of white card stock. Using a pencil, trace around the photograph. Set the photograph aside.

3. Cut the apple down the center and set aside. Cut the lemon lengthwise and the lime down the center.

4. Follow instructions for **Object Prints** on page 24.

   Hint: You will want some of the fruit to slightly overlap the pencil sketched photograph area.

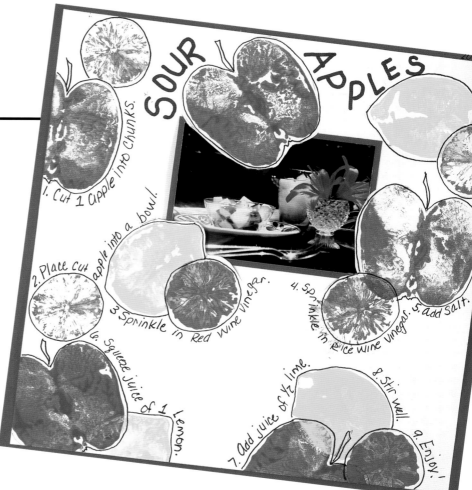

5. Let the paint dry completely.

6. Using a utility knife, carefully cut around the fruit that overlaps the pencil-sketched photograph area. Place the photograph behind the overlapping fruit.

7. Using a pencil, sketch around each fruit stamp. Write the title of the recipe at the top of the layout page and the steps to the recipe around the fruit. Trace over pencil with a marker.

P R O J E C T

At My Daddy's Office

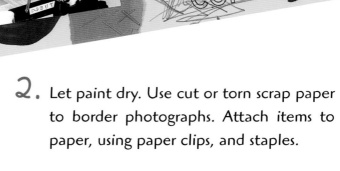

Project Tools & Materials

- Alphabet stickers
- Card stock
- Hot-glue gun
- Office stamps
- Paper clips
- Paper scraps
- Pencil
- Photographs
- Stamp pad
- Stapler

Instructions

1. Use office stamps and acrylic paint to print on card stock and follow instructions for **Object Prints** on page 24. Do not worry about being too neat.

2. Let paint dry. Use cut or torn scrap paper to border photographs. Attach items to paper, using paper clips, and staples.

3. Using alphabet stickers, add narration onto page.

   Hint: Add words such as *Confidential* and *Copy* around photographs.

4. Adhere pencil onto page, using a hot-glue gun.

Learning My Numbers

• To make prints using numbers such as the print shown below, place number stickers around the page. Then using a brayer, roll black and white ink over the number stickers. Remove number stickers after ink has dried. The result will be a reverse object print.

Hint: Be certain to test a number on a piece of scrap paper first. If the adhesive is too strong, stick it on your hand a few times to remove some of the stickiness.

Mom, This Is the Best!

• Repeat steps from **Sour Apples** on page 25, using an artichoke instead of fruit. The leaves of the artichoke make an interesting print on the page.

ARTICHOKES

Artichoke
PEPPER
PAPriKA
BAY LEAF
PARLSEY

YUM

1. Fill a pot With WAter.

2. Add a BayleaF, paprika, pepper, and an artichoke.

3. Boil until tender.

4. chill in refrigerator.

5. Serve with parsley

2003

P R O J E C T

Nature Printing

- Follow the instructions for making **Object Prints** on page 24. Use hosta leaves to make beautiful leafy prints. The large-veined leaves are perfect for printing.

- Use three leaves and stamp each in a different color of paint. Do not forget to overlap the leaves with different colors of paint.

Styrofoam Prints

TECHNIQUE

Styrofoam prints are easy to do. Get Styrofoam trays from your local butcher. Always use the flat back side of the trays.

Technique Tools & Materials

Acrylic paint

Card stock

Paintbrush

Scissors

Sharpened pencil

Styrofoam

Instructions

1. Cut large pieces of Styrofoam into circles or squares to make them more workable.

2. Using a sharpened pencil, carve an image into the Styrofoam.

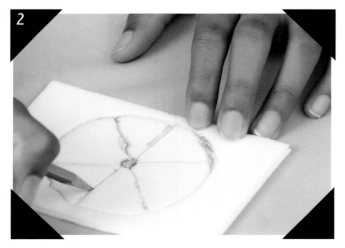

Hint: Use a glass to form a perfect circle in the Styrofoam.

3. Using a paintbrush, cover carved image with paint.

4. Place painted Styrofoam stamp face down onto card stock and press lightly.

5. Press down with more force when printing a second or third time.

6. Add more paint onto Styrofoam stamp and repeat stamping process until you are finished.

PROJECT

Sour Lemon Face

Project Tools & Materials

Alphabet stickers

Dark green scrap paper

Juice glass

Photographs

Instructions

1. To make the lemon print, place the juice glass in the center of a 4" piece of Styrofoam. Press down firmly to make an impression.

2. Using a pencil, trace around the circle to make the impression more defined.

3. Make a small circle in the center of the large circle and then make straight lines from one edge of the circle to the other. Be certain to make the lines go through the circle's center.

4. Follow the instructions for making **Styrofoam Prints** on page 30.

5. Crop and border photographs of your friends making funny faces after eating a lemon.

PROJECT

Puppet Show

- Follow instructions for making **Styrofoam Prints** on page 30. Print Styrofoam prints on white paper. Cut out prints and glue them onto colored paper backgrounds.

- It's fun to make your prints resemble an object from the photograph.

TREEHOUSE

SPRING 2003

Double Trouble

• Draw a pack of gum on the Styrofoam with *Double Trouble* on it. Follow the instructions for making **Styrofoam Prints** on page 30.

Hints: To make your prints match the prints on this page, use turquoise paint on the words and lighter green on the package.

• Remember, you are making a print; so if you sketch normal letters into the Styrofoam, they will appear backwards.

What I Like/Dislike

• Follow the instructions for making **Styrofoam Prints** on page 30 to make prints of things you like and things that you dislike.

• Ask a friend, sibling, or parent to take a photograph of you making two different faces. The first one experiencing something very good and the other experiencing something very bad.

• If you make a scrapbook page like this every few years, you will see your likes and dislikes change as you grow up.

How Does Your Garden Grow?

• Follow the instructions for making **Stryofoam Prints** on page 30.

• One of the best things about Styrofoam printing stamps is they can be used over again. This technique is perfect for making background patterns. It is fun to use various colors of paper to see how the paint blends.

• Stamp rows of prints to resemble the rows of plants in a garden. Wash the Styrofoam with water when switching paint colors.

Glue-line Prints

TECHNIQUE

This technique is a simple way of making prints, and the concept is similar to the process involved in printing newspapers and books. The lines may join, run parallel, twist, and crisscross to create a visual reaction.

Hints: The ink dries very fast so work quickly. Don't worry about washing the brayer in between ink applications. It will take too much time. It's okay if the color bleeds through.

• Once you have made your print and the ink has dried, follow the instructions for making **Tin Foil Relief** on pages 42–43. You'll have a whole new look.

Word to Know

Transparent means to be clear. If an object is transparent you can see through it.

Technique Tools & Materials

Brayer
Card stock
Pencil
Plastic plate
School glue
Spray bottle of water
Water-soluble ink

Instructions

1. To make a glue-line printing plate, sketch desired image onto card stock. A certain amount of detail is needed, but lines too close together will result in lines of glue running together forming one thick line.

2. Using glue, trace over all pencil lines in the sketch. Glue is completely dried when it becomes transparent.

   Hint: Open lid on your school glue, slightly. This will help control flow of glue.

3. Squeeze a quarter-sized dab of ink onto plastic plate and roll it out smooth, using brayer.

4. Cover entire glue-line page with ink, then quickly place a sheet of card stock onto glue-line plate. Ink dries very quickly so have card stock ready. A spray bottle of water will help keep the ink tacky.

5. Remove card stock from inked plate to reveal the print.

P R O J E C T

Spooky Halloween

Project Tools & Materials

Black card stock
Black marker
Halloween-patterned paper
Photographs
Transfer paper
White scrap paper

Instructions

1. Follow the instructions for making **Glue-line Prints** on page 36 and above.

2. Sketch a large ghost onto a piece of scrap card stock.

3. Write *Boo* onto a piece of scrap paper, using a black marker. Lay the transfer paper (graphite-side down) onto the sketch. Place the word *Boo* right side down on the transfer paper. Image should look backward. Using a pencil, trace over the word and remove transfer paper.

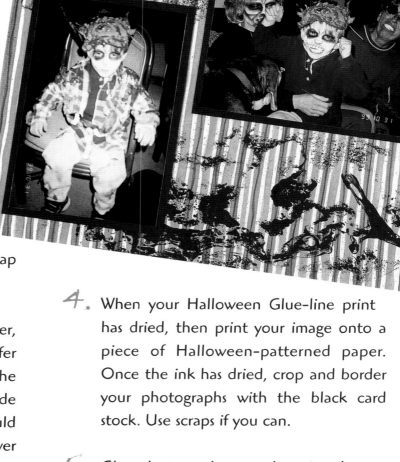

4. When your Halloween Glue-line print has dried, then print your image onto a piece of Halloween-patterned paper. Once the ink has dried, crop and border your photographs with the black card stock. Use scraps if you can.

5. Glue photographs onto the printed page.

PROJECT

On the Way to the Beach

• To begin this project, sketch seashells and starfish onto the card stock. Then follow the instructions for making **Glue-line Prints** on pages 36–37. Let the glue dry completely.

• This page uses three colors of ink to get the multicolored effect.

PROJECT

Life on the Scit Scat

• Sketch an anchor and waves before making this glue-line print. Follow the instructions for **Glue-line Prints** on pages 36–37, using blue ink.

• To finish, border your photograph with blue and yellow card stock before gluing it onto the page.

Life on the Scit Scat

PROJECT

Turtle at the Zoo

• To make this page, sketch a picture of your favorite animal at the zoo and then follow the instructions for making **Glue-line Prints** on pages 36–37.

P R O J E C T

Taking a Hike

- To make this page, sketch abstract images onto a piece of card stock.

 Word to Know

Abstract means consisting of unidentifiable shapes and figures.

- Follow the instructions for **Glue-line Prints** on pages 36–37. Print the image onto green card stock using black ink. Then, while the ink is still wet, apply brown ink.

Tin Foil Relief

TECHNIQUE

Tin Foil Reliefs are dramatic and powerful. Children of all ages like this project.

Hints: Use heavy-duty tin foil if you can, if you use regular foil, be careful not to tear it with your pencil. You may want to use a cotton swab and your fingers instead.

• When you make your projects, you may want to use only one color of shoe polish instead of two or three, or have simple details rather than a complex image.

Technique Tools & Materials

Black shoe polish
Card stock
Heavy-duty tin foil
Paintbrush
Paper towels
Pencil
School glue

Instructions

1. Follow instructions for making **Glue-line Prints** on pages 36–37 and make picture.

2. When glue becomes transparent, pour two tablespoons glue into a small bowl and dilute with one tablespoon water.

3. Tear off a piece of heavy-duty tin foil at least 4" larger than glue-line print.

4. Using a paintbrush, spread glue evenly over the entire surface of picture.

5. Place tin foil over picture and firmly rub flat with fingers.

6. Begin tracing around glue lines using a dull pencil. Add texture by scribbling gently over entire relief picture in all directions.

Detail of Tin Foil Relief.

7. Turn picture over and glue excess tin foil to back side of relief picture.

8. Apply shoe polish to entire front surface of tin foil. Allow shoe polish to dry for a few minutes. Lightly rub across relief picture with paper towel to remove excess polish from tin foil.

Hint: If desired, follow the same procedure using brown and blue shoe polish to further stain the tin foil.

PROJECT

Playin' in the Sand

Project Tools & Materials

Black card stock
Black scrap paper
Mounting adhesive
Photographs

Instructions

1. Use the same printing plate you used for **On the Way to the Beach** on page 38.

2. Follow instructions for making **Tin Foil Relief** on page 42 and above.

3. Apply mounting adhesive onto the back side of the tin foil relief and adhere it onto the center of a black piece of card stock.

4. Border your photographs, using black scrap paper. Glue them onto the page.

P R O J E C T

ANCHORS AWAY

• You can make this page by using the **Life on the Scit Scat** project on page 39. Then, follow instructions for making **Tin Foil Relief** on pages 42–43.

• The goal of this page is to create the idea the anchor is old and has begun to patina. Use brown and blue shoe polish to create this look.

 **Word to Know**

Patina means a thin layer of corrosion, usually brown or green, that appears on metal.

Wonders of Nature

This page also uses a glue-line print project as its base.

- Follow the instructions for making the **Take a Hike** project on page 41. Then follow the instructions for making **Tin Foil Relief** on pages 42–43. Border the relief and your photographs using two coordinating colors of card stock.

PROJECT
Halloween

• When you make two pages that go together, you can showcase more pictures. You can display the scrapbook pages here and on page 47 either together or alone.

• Just follow the instructions for making the **Tin Foil Relief** on pages 42–43, using the colors shown here.

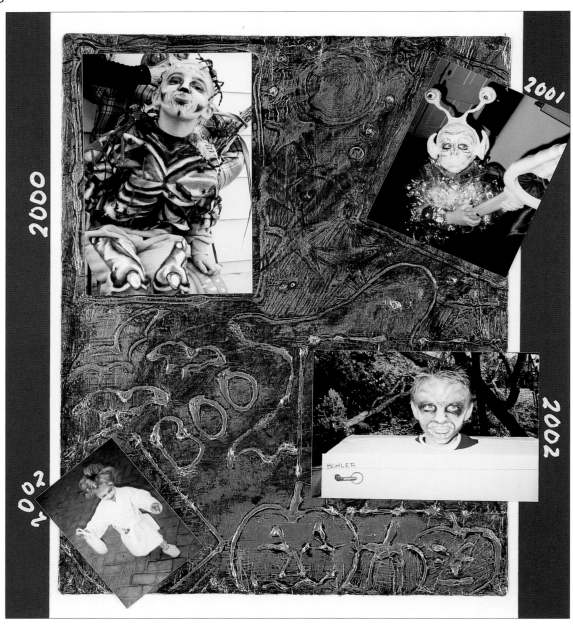

• Include photographs from a couple of years of Halloween costumes. Then you can look back later and laugh at how silly or great your costume was that year.

2001

2001

2002

Acrylic Layers

TECHNIQUE

Almost anything goes when making Acrylic Layers, but watching the paint move and dry is especially interesting for most children.

Hints: Use an old towel or newspapers to cover work area. When air from the hair drier hits the paint, it will splatter and run off the sides of the paper.

• Gel medium comes in different finishes. Gel matte means it will dry with a dull finish. Gel gloss dries with a shiny finish. In addition, the more Gel you add, the more transparent the colors will become. The amount of water added to the paint mixture will determine how runny the paint will become. Experiment and find the look you like.

Technique Tools & Materials

Acrylic gel medium
Acrylic paints (3 colors)
Hair drier
Plastic cup
Spray bottle filled with water
White card stock

Instructions

1. In a plastic cup, add gel medium to paint. Dilute with water and mix well.

2. Drizzle first color of paint over a large portion of card stock.

3. Spray card stock with water, creating small puddles.

4. Use a hair drier to blow paint across card stock until paint has completely dried.

5. Continue procedure with each color.

PROJECT

Mask Making

Project Tools & Materials

Glue

Markers: fine, thick

Pencil

Photographs

Ribbons: purple, red

Scrap papers: purple, red, yellow

Instructions

1. Follow instructions for making **Acrylic Layers** on page 48. Let page dry completely.

2. Border photographs with purple, red, or yellow. Glue photographs onto page.

3. Using a pencil, sketch masks around the page. Using a marker, trace the masks and color inside the lines.

   Hint: To draw the mask, just draw two teardrops touching each other.

4. Cut two 10" strips of ribbon. Tie them together with a knot in the center. Place a dot of glue on one edge of each mask and press the knot down into the glue.

5. Cut a rectangle from scraps and narrate.

Crazy Grammy & Her Brothers

Sometimes it is nice to make a scrapbook page look very old. It is not hard to do, just follow the instructions.

 Word to Know

Antiquing means to make something appear old.

Hint: When the doily is wet, it becomes very fragile and rips easily. Don't worry about it too much because when objects get old, they tend to rip and tear easily. This could be the added touch to make your doily look old.

Project Tools & Materials

10" doily
Brown acrylic paint
Card stocks: brown, bright pink
Clear adhesive-backed bumpers (4)
Decorative-edged scissors
Glue stick
Gel medium
Large paintbrush
Old photograph
Photo corners
Pie plate
Plastic dinner plate
Tea bags
White ribbon

Instructions

1. Using a large paintbrush, mix brown acrylic paint with gel medium on plastic dinner plate.

2. Brush brown paint thickly onto pink card stock, with brush strokes going from top to bottom. Cover entire paper with paint.

3. Using hair drier, dry paper completely.

4. Turn paper and apply paint thickly, with brush strokes going the opposite direction.

5. Let paper dry completely.

6. Fill pie plate ¼ full of warm water. Add several tea bags and allow bags to soak in the water until it turns brown.

7. Remove tea bags and lay doily and ribbon in water until they become brown. This will make them appear old. Remove carefully and allow to dry on a flat surface. Hair drier may be used to speed drying process.

8. Draw 10½" circle on brown card stock. Cut out circle with decorative-edged scissors.

9. Glue brown circle onto background paper. Glue doily onto brown circle. The old photograph should not be glued onto doily, but be placed in photo corners to avoid damaging it.

10. Cut two holes through doily and background paper for ribbon. Thread ribbon through holes and tie in a bow.

11. Attach clear adhesive-backed bumpers onto corners of background to protect ribbon from being damaged by other scrapbook pages.

I Love Fruits & Veggies

• To re-create this page, follow the instructions for **Acrylic Layers** on page 48 and use fall-like colors and leaves from your yard. After you use the hair drier to spread the paint onto the page. To make the leaf prints, press leaves into the wet paint and remove to reveal the leaf impression.

PROJECT

Going Out to Dinner

- Follow the instructions for making **Acrylic Layers** on page 48, using paints that correspond to the colors in your photographs.

- To make the page shiny, on the final layer, use a paintbrush to add a thick layer of copper paint over the entire page. Comb through wet paint, using a hair pick.

- To add wire onto your page, poke holes in the page with a needle. Thread one end of your wire through the page and curl the other around the top of a pen or a bottle top.

Bubble Paper

TECHNIQUE

Toddlers have a great time blowing bubbles and capturing the bubble images on paper.

Technique Tools & Materials

Drinking glass

Flexible straw

Food coloring or water soluble ink

Liquid dish soap

Towel, plastic dinner plate, or rag

Water

White card stock

Instructions

1. Fill a drinking glass with water and food coloring.

2. Add one drop liquid dish soap.

   Hint: Make certain to only use one drop of dish soap, in case someone accidentally swallows bubble mixture while blowing through straw.

3. Place glass on top of towel, plastic dinner plate, or rag since bubbles tend to overflow glass. Insert a flexible straw and begin blowing until bubbles form above the rim of glass.

4. Quickly place card stock over bubbles, then remove.

5. Continue blowing bubbles and placing card stock over bubbles until entire paper is covered with bubble imprints.

Shaving Cream War

Project Tools & Materials

- Alphabet stickers
- Glue stick
- Patterned paper
- Photographs
- Solid-colored card stock

Instructions

1. Follow instructions for making **Bubble Paper** on page 54, using black food coloring or ink. Let bubbles dry completely.

2. Cut out different-sized bubble shapes. Arrange the cut out bubbles around the photographs and glue into place.

3. Glue bubbles and photographs onto a solid-colored card stock and cut a small border.

4. Glue photographs with bubble and border onto patterned paper. Narrate using alphabet stickers.

Blowing Bubbles

Have fun experimenting with the look and feel of black-and-white photographs. Photographs of your friends capturing bubbles in the air make great scrapbook pages.

• To make this page, follow the instructions for making **Bubble Paper** on page 54, using black food coloring. Border the photographs with black paper and use gray or black alphabet stickers to narrate the page.

• You don't need black-and-white film. Use regular film and let the developer know you would like it printed in black and white when you drop it off for processing.

Sitting in the tub

1996

P R O J E C T

Sitting in the Tub

Safety Note: Never place supporting hand in front of knife. Adults will need to supervise this activity.

• Make **Bubble Paper**, following the instructions on page 54. To put your photograph behind the bubbles, place your photograph in the center of the bubble paper and lightly trace around it with a pencil. Using a utility knife, cut an X into the center of the rectangle.

• Following the flow of the bubbles, cut a small window out in the center of the rectangle. Place the photograph behind the bubble in the center of the window.

6-17-03

P R O J E C T

WASHING THE DOG

• Make your **Bubble Paper** following the instructions on page 54. To make your bubbles sparkle just like the bubbles in the picture, each time you place the card stock over the bubbles, quickly sprinkle glitter over the bubbles while they are still wet.

• In this picture, the photographs are cut into the shape of bubbles as well.

SURFING IN THE HOT TUB

• To make this page, use brown food coloring when making your **Bubble Paper** following the instructions on page 54. Using a white marker, sketch bubbles on dark brown card stock and cut out around them. Place these bubbles around your photograph.

• Narrate the page around the bubbles.

Watercolor Designs

TECHNIQUE

Children of all ages have a great time painting with watercolors. The best part is that it washes out easily.

Hints: You may wish to invest in professional grade watercolors because the colors are much richer.

• Since children always want a new sheet of paper when they make a mistake, tear watercolor paper into sections. To tear paper more easily but still keep the beautiful ripped edges, use a metal yardstick and score the paper where you want the tear to run.

Technique Tools & Materials

Glass of water
Watercolor paints
Watercolor paper
Wide paintbrush

Instructions

1. Moisten paints with water and set aside.

2. Using wide paintbrush, quickly brush water across watercolor paper, making certain not to cover entire page. Leave some edges dry and run water off others.

3. Select several colors of paint and begin adding color to page. Distribute each color in at least three different areas.

Hint: Watercolors will begin to run in various directions and some will combine to make new colors.

4. When watercolor has dried, place several books on top of paper to press it flat.

P R O J E C T

Chick Chat

Project Tools & Materials

Card stocks: navy, tan
Pencil
Photographs
Small paintbrush
Tan scrap paper

Instructions

1. Sketch an egg with a crack in it onto the watercolor paper. Then follow the instructions for **Watercolor Designs** on page 60.

2. Paint the sky around the egg. Let the sky dry completely. Paint the earth, using shades of green and brown.

3. Let the paper dry completely. Border each photograph with tan card stock and glue onto the navy card stock.

   Hint: To make your border edges a little jagged, fold the paper into the desired size and tear, instead of trimming, the edges against a countertop or table edge.

4. Narrate the page, using watercolors.

WHERE
I
WANT
TO
BE

2003

P R O J E C T

Where I Want to Be

• This page is really simple. Just follow instructions for **Watercolor Designs** on page 60. Then border your photographs, glue them onto the watercolor paper, and apply alphabet stickers onto the page for narration.

• This project is a great way to remember your first bedroom or house.

Our House

• Follow the instructions for making **Watercolor Designs** on page 60. Glue the photographs onto the page and sketch around each photograph with a marker.

• One idea is to sketch an extension of the photograph. Remember to let the marker flow naturally. This will help your sketches look more artistic.

PROJECT

Now We're Cookin'

• Follow the instructions for making **Watercolor Designs** on page 60. Color-in your sketches with watercolors and let them dry before gluing photographs onto the page.

• If you don't like to cook, try using photographs of you making this project and sketch art supplies.

2003

MY FIRST

FIRST

TEA PARTY

2003

MY FIRST TEA PARTY

• To make this page, follow the instructions for **Watercolor Designs** on page 60. This time, color-in the sketches with colored pencils.

Word to Know

Mixed media. To complete this project, you will use more than one medium. Using watercolors is one medium and colored pencils are another medium. Together, you have a page with mixed media. (Media is the plural form of medium.)

Chalk Shavings

TECHNIQUE

Ages 6 and up

Safety Note: Adults will need to supervise this activity when spraying varathane.

Hint: Sidewalk chalk works great for this technique because it's easier for small hands to hold and less likely to break.

Word to Know

When you use a **silhouette** on the page, it is the same as a shadow of the image you are using.

Technique Tools & Materials

Card stocks: black, other colors
Chalk or pastels
Cookie sheet
Glue
Grater
Pencil
Water
Varathane spray

Instructions

1. Pour enough water into a cookie sheet to cover bottom of pan.

2. Select desired colors of chalk and grate chalk over water.

3. Lay a piece of card stock on top of the water and gently press down over the entire paper so the chalk adheres onto the paper. Let the paper dry completely.

Hint: If you are using colored pastels, press down firmly over entire paper or slide the paper underneath the floating pastels. This will help the pastels adhere to the paper.

4. When paper is completely dry, spray a thin layer of varathane over the entire surface to prevent the chalk from rubbing off.

5. Using a pencil or white chalk, sketch images onto a black piece of card stock.

6. Cut out the images and glue them onto the chalk paper to create a silhouette.

Hints: An accidental cut through part of a silhouette is not important. When glued, the mistake will be hidden.

- Do not worry about pencil lines. They add a nice effect. Additional lines may be drawn for more detail.

- It is sometimes difficult to get photographs to adhere to chalk paper. It helps to place photograph tape onto both the image and chalk paper.

PROJECT

Yellowstone

Project Tools & Materials
Photographs
Scrap paper
Yellow marker

Instructions

1. Follow instructions for making **Chalk Shavings** on page 66 and above.

2. Sketch cliffs, bluffs, pine trees, and clouds onto black card stock, then cut out images.

3. Crop and border photographs with scrap paper and glue them onto the chalk paper.

4. Glue silhouette images onto chalk paper, overlapping some of the photographs.

5. Using a yellow marker, narrate the page.

FALL 1998

PROJECT

My Bike

• To make this page, follow the instructions for making **Chalk Shavings** on pages 66–67, using blue, green, orange, peach, purple, red, and yellow chalk. Sketch clouds and houses onto black card stock, cut them out and glue them onto the page.

P R O J E C T

What a Great Day!

- Follow the instructions for making **Chalk Shavings** on pages 66–67, using earth tones. Make silhouettes of a boat, tree, shore, and sun. Use alphabet letters to narrate the page.

 Words to Know

Earth Tones are any rich color containing brown.

- This page is a great way to remember a day you spent with a special family member. It would make a great birthday gift, too.

My Family Tree

• To make the family tree pages shown above, you'll need to gather photographs of your family members. Be certain that the photographs are small enough that they will all fit onto the page.

• Follow the instructions for making **Chalk Shavings** on pages 66–67. You will need to make two pages, one for each side of your family. Place two pieces of black card stock together and sketch your tree. Half of the tree should be on each piece of paper.

PROJECT

Under the Trellis

• Follow the instructions for **Chalk Shavings** on pages 66–67. While the chalk paper is drying, sketch a trellis onto black card stock and cut it out. Make certain it takes up most of the page so that a photograph can fit inside. To make the vine that wraps around the trellis, place your trellis onto a piece of black scrap paper. Use this as a guide for making the vine.

Photograph Pockets

TECHNIQUE

This is a fun and unique technique for putting several similar pictures together. The photographs are in their own little pocket or handmade envelope. To make the pocket, you might want to substitute the doily with a 10" circle cut from paper.

Technique Tools & Materials

10" paper doily

Hole punch

Needle

Pencil

Ribbon

Scissors

Instructions

1. Carefully fold each side of the doily toward the center about 1".

   Hint: When using a doily for your pocket, be careful because they tear easily.

2. Fold the top and bottom of the doily inward, making certain the top flap overlaps the bottom flap slightly.

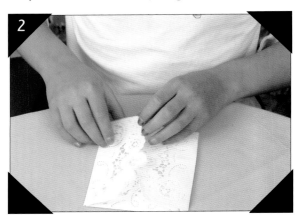

3. Thread a needle with ribbon and press the needle down through the bottom flap of your pocket. Run the needle back up through the paper.

4. Close the pocket. Using a pencil, make a small dot on the top flap directly over the underlying ribbon. Punch a hole over the pencil mark.

5. Thread the ribbon through the hole and tie into a bow.

⟦P⟧⟦R⟧⟦O⟧⟦J⟧⟦E⟧⟦C⟧⟦T⟧

Hugs & Kisses

Project Tools & Materials

Blue card stock
Marker
Photo tape
Photographs

Instructions

1. Follow instructions for making **Photo-graph Pockets** on page 72.

2. Place photo tape onto the back side of the closed pocket and press it firmly into place on the layout page.

3. Cut your photographs into the shape of hearts and then glue them onto the solid blue card stock. Cut around the photograph so you have a heart-shaped border around each.

4. Thread a 36" piece of the red ribbon through the needle and through each photograph to make a chain.

5. Thread the ribbon through the left corner of the envelope. Place photographs in the envelope and tie it shut with a bow.

6. Using a 12" piece of white ribbon, fold the ribbon in half and cut out a half of a heart shape.

7. Follow the process of cutting hearts across the length of the ribbon.

8. Cut out hearts of various sizes into the card stock. Glue the ribbon and hearts onto the card stock.

9. Using a marker, narrate the page.

Flowers

Project Tools & Materials

Alphabet stickers

Foam flowers

Glue stick

Patterned paper

Photographs

Instructions

1. Glue a large piece of patterned paper approximately 8" x 7" onto the page.

2. Place your stack of photographs into the center of the patterned paper and trace around lightly with a pencil. Set photographs aside.

3. Begin gluing flowers around the bottom corners of the pencil drawing, making certain to only glue the outer sides of the flowers. This will create a pocket in which to set your photographs.

4. Glue additional flowers around the page to add interest. Slip your stack of photographs into the pocket.

5. Narrate the page using alphabet stickers.

P R O J E C T

Surprise Inside

• To make this page, follow the instructions for making **Photograph Pockets** on page 72. Draw and cut two circles from scrap papers, using a salad plate and a bread plate as templates. Glue the smaller circle inside of the larger circle.

Word to Know

A **template** is a pattern for your project.

• Adhere the photograph into the center of the circles before folding. This way you will be certain that the photograph is inside of the creases and the pocket will fold correctly.

P R O J E C T

Flowers, Buttons & Bows

Project Tools & Materials

Book bone

Flower button

Glue stick

Needle

Papers, corresponding colors (5)

Photographs

Ruler

Instructions

1. To make the pocket, cut one 9" x 12" piece from paper.

2. Turn the paper vertically. Measure 4" up from the bottom edge. Using a book bone, run a straight line horizontally.

3. Fold the paper at the line. Then turning the paper around, measure in 2" from each corner toward the center of page.

4. Placing the ruler on a diagonal over the 2" mark, run a straight line across each corner of the paper.

5. Fold over each corner at the line, then glue corners down.

6. Thread a large needle with 20" of ribbon, then push the needle through the top, center edge of the envelope. Push the thread back through the bottom of paper.

7. Thread another piece of ribbon 5" long up through the center of the bottom flap (the needle will be going from the inside of the envelope outward). Then thread through the front of the paper and back through the paper again.

8. Tie the ribbon in a snug knot.

9. Using another 8" x 11" piece of colored paper, measure in 2" from each top corner and make pin-sized pencil mark.

10. Measure down 2" on each side of the paper and make a mark. Then, using a ruler, draw a diagonal line joining the two dots. Trim off both corners of the paper.

11. Glue paper in the center of the inside of the envelope.

12. Once you have followed the instructions above and completed the envelope, you are ready to assemble the layout page.

13. Put glue on the back side of the envelope and adhere in center of the layout page you have selected.

14. Sketch and cut out flowers using paper with different colors and patterns, then glue onto the paper and envelope.

15. Remember to make creases using the book bone on any flowers overlapping the envelope. This will ensure a crisp crease when opening the envelope.

16. Crop and border photographs with remaining paper. Place photographs inside the envelope and tie shut.

Mosaic Scraps

Ages 5 and up

This technique is a creative way of using scrap paper to make interesting designs and patterns. Either tear or cut the paper into small pieces. Once children can manipulate scissors or tear small pieces of paper, this is a fun way to help develop their dexterity and motor skills.

Hint: When using more than one pattern or color of paper, it helps to keep each pattern or color in a separate pile.

 Word to Know

A **mosaic** is a picture or decorative design made by setting small colored pieces onto another surface.

Technique Tools & Materials
Card stock
Glue stick
Scissors
Scrap papers

Instructions
1. Cut or tear papers into small pieces.

2. Sketch design onto card stock.

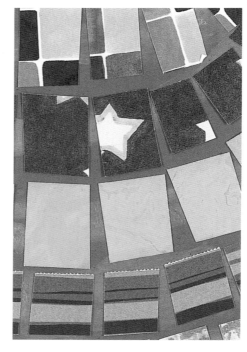

Detail of patterned mosaic pieces.

3. Run a thick line of glue about 6" long over the pencil line.

4. Place paper scraps onto the glue line. Leave a small space between each piece.

5. Once glue line is covered, make another line of glue and continue pasting down scraps until all pencil lines and areas to be filled in are finished.

6. Follow the same procedure on every pencil line.

PROJECT

my firsts

Project Tools & Materials

Marker

Photographs

Instructions

1. Follow instructions for making **Mosaic Scraps** on page 78.

2. Using a pencil, write in large, thick letters *My Firsts* and draw two flowers and a long strip of grass onto the black card stock.

3. Glue the scraps of paper to fill in the letters, flowers, and grass.

4. Cut out the letters and objects and glue them on a piece of card stock.

5. Crop and border photographs with black card stock and adhere onto card stock.

6. Using a marker, narrate the page.

Baseball

Spring 2002

- To make this scrapbook page, follow the instructions for **Mosaic Scraps** on page 78 and form a spiral with the glue. Add scraps starting from the outside and moving inward.

- Use a page color that coordinates with the team colors.

PROJECT

Best Buds

• To make this two-page spread, place two sheets of card stock next to each other. Using a pencil, draw wavy lines across each page. Be certain that they flow across both pages. Make more than one line. Then follow the instructions for **Mosaic Scraps** on page 78.

• Using a two-page spread is a great idea when you have quite a few photographs that you want to showcase.

Colored Pencil Cutouts

TECHNIQUE

This is the perfect opportunity for you and your friends to take crazy pictures.

Safety Note: Never place supporting hand in front of utility knife. Adults will need to supervise this activity.

Hint: Use photographs of facial expressions to create direction and flow. Placing a photograph that is looking downward and to the left at the top-left side of the page will make the eye movement flow in that direction.

Technique Tools & Materials

Black graphite transfer paper
Colored pencils
Light-colored card stock
Photo tape
Photographs
Scissors
Utility knife

Instructions

1. Begin by placing the photographs onto the page in the direction you want them to face.

2. Place the transfer paper onto a piece of card stock. Lay the photographs over the transfer paper and using a pencil, sketch around the face.

3. Remove the photograph and transfer paper and you will have an outline of the face. Make an X in the center of outline of face, using a utility knife.

4. Stick one scissor blade through the hole and cut out the outline.

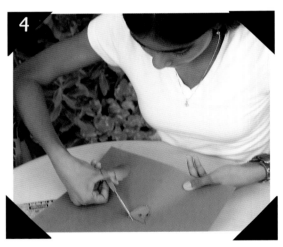

5. Turn over the paper and place photo tape around the entire edge of the cut-out image.

6. Place the cut-out paper over the photograph, then cut off any areas of the photograph that show.

7. Using colored pencils, draw a funny character to go with the face.

8. Continue the same process with each photograph.

Roller-coaster Ride

Project Tools & Materials

Pencil

Hint: Ask your friends to make faces for photographs like they are riding on a roller coaster. Have some look forward and others look toward the side.

Instructions

1. Using a pencil, make a basic sketch of a roller coaster.

2. Follow instructions for **Colored Pencil Cutouts** on page 82 and adhere a photograph of each person riding in the roller coaster.

3. Using a pencil, draw bodies to each face.

4. Using colored pencils, color-in all images.

P R O J E C T

A Day at the Lake

- Follow the instructions for making **Colored Pencil Cutouts** on page 82.

- Use your imagination, try making a mermaid or a man-eating fish.

A Dog's Life

• After making the page, following the instructions for making **Colored Pencil Cutouts** on page 82, sketch human bodies and add dog faces. Sketch dog bodies and add the faces of you and your friends.

Togetherness

- Have a parent or friend take a photograph of you with your sister, brother, or friend sitting next to one another. Then take a close-up photograph of your pet. Follow the instructions for making **Colored Pencil Cutouts** on page 82.

- Imagine a place you would like to go and use that place as the scenery around the automobile.

PROJECT

I'm Athletic

• If you love to play sports, this is the perfect page to showcase your talents.

• Follow the instructions for **Colored Pencil Cutouts** on page 82. Sketch drawings of bodies playing different sports and then add photographs of yourself.

Pullouts

TECHNIQUE

This technique takes some extra thinking and planning before beginning the project. Just follow the instructions and use the hints below to make the projects work smoothly.

Hints: Throughout the process lay your pop-up images onto the layout page. This will help you to visualize how to make it work.

• To save time and money, purchase brads of one color. If you need it to be a different color, just add a dot of paint onto the top.

• You may need to lay the images onto your layout page to determine the best place to put the lever.

• Another trick is figuring out where to put the glue so you can adhere it onto the layout page. It must be placed on the image where it won't interfere with the motion of the lever.

Technique Tools & Materials
Brads or fasteners
Card stock
Glue stick
Scissors

Instructions

1. Sketch images onto card stock.

2. Using scissors, cut out the images.

3. If one image is to pull out from behind another, make certain the front image is large enough to conceal the second image when tucked behind.

4. Once all images are cut out, cut a long strip of card stock 1" wide.

5. Press brad through center of the largest image, then press brad through long card-stock strip. This enables the smaller image to pivot up and down.

6. Glue pullout or smaller image onto strip of card stock. Lay out small image the way you want it to look. This helps to determine where on the strip to glue pullout image.

Diggers & Dump Trucks

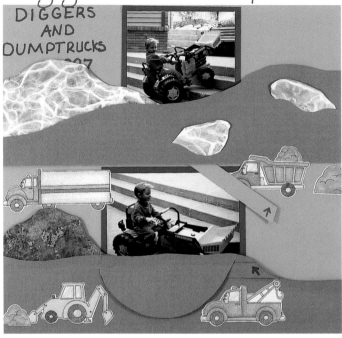

Project Tools & Materials

Card stock: dirt- or sand-colored

Crayons

Photographs

Scissors

Scrap paper

Instructions

1. Follow the instructions for making **Pullouts** on page 88. Position photograph onto card stock. Leave room for rock and dirt.

2. Cut strip of card stock for lever. Make paper rock and glue onto one end of lever.

3. Find a pivot point on background paper and lever so the rock will move the way you want it to move. Attach lever to background with brad.

4. Cut sand- or dirt-colored card stock so the rock will have a place to both start and finish with the lever movement.

5. Lever may go under sand-colored paper or through cutout. Glue items in place and decorate as desired.

PROJECT

Signing Hands

• To make this page, use the instructions from **Object Prints** on page 24 to make your handprint. Then follow the instructions for making **Pullouts** on page 88. Thread fishing line through each fingertip, separately to make that finger movable.

• This project would be great to make about a friend who knows sign language. They could help you to position the fingers correctly.

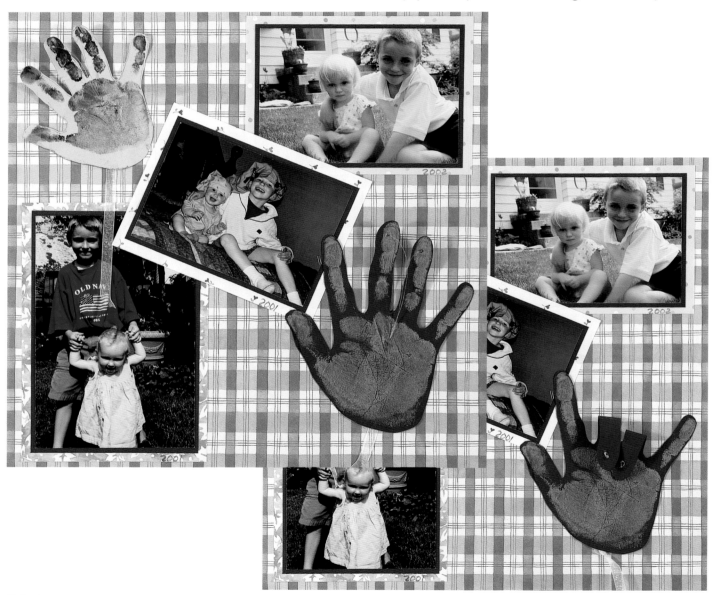

P R O J E C T
Everything's Blooming

• To make the pullout flowers in this project, follow the instructions for making **Pullouts** on page 88. Cut out everything for the page. Attach six flower stems together and accordion-fold the stems of the bottom flowers so that they can be hidden inside the pot.

• This project is great for younger scrapbookers because it uses large basic shapes that are easy to handle and recognize.

PROJECT
At the Ranch

Safety Note: Never place supporting hand in front of utility knife. Adults will need to supervise this activity.

Project Tools & Materials

Crayons
Photographs
Scrap paper
Utility knife

Instructions

1. Follow the instructions for **Pullouts** on page 88. Then follow instructions 2–7 here to make cutouts and tabs.

2. To make the barn door open, cut three sides with a utility knife.

3. To make the horse in the barn move, crop and border the photograph. Glue a long strip of lime-green card stock to the middle of the photograph.

4. Place the photograph where you would like it to come out of the barn. Gently pull the photograph out of the barn and make a mark where you want it to stop.

5. Using the utility knife, make a small vertical slit in the card stock along the width of the lime-green strip. Make another slit the same length about 2" to the left.

6. Feed the line-green strip down through the left slit and up through the right slit. cut away any strip that may hang over the side of the layout page.

7. Repeat instructions 2–6 with a second photograph behind the fences at the top of the page.

![P] ![R] ![O] ![J] ![E] ![C] ![T]

Where's the Easter Bunny?

Project Tools & Materials

Brads

Card stocks: blue, green, white

Patterned paper

Photographs

Scissors

Scrap paper

Instructions

1. Follow the instructions for **Pullouts** on page 88.

2. To make the bunny, make circles for the head, back side, and tail of the bunny. Make two triangles for the feet.

3. Draw two waterdrops for the ears. To make the ears look droopy, make another waterdrop on one side of each ear. Sketch in the face using a pencil. Color with black and pink markers and cut out all of the shapes.

4. Cut a strip from the green paper and glue it horizontally behind the bunny's face. Press a brad through the center of the bunny's body, then through the green strip 1" from its face. Glue the bunny's feet onto the patterned paper.

5. To make the sun and cloud, sketch a cloud onto white scrap paper and cut out. Trace another circle onto a piece of yellow scrap paper and cut out.

6. Cut a strip from blue paper and glue it behind the center of the yellow circle. Make a small arrow on the tip of the strip with a different colored marker. This will show which direction to slide the trip.

7. Press a brad through the top-center of the cloud. Glue the right side of the cloud onto the page.

Crayon Etching

Ages 5 and up

Etching into crayon produces a very dramatic look. Be careful not to use too much crayon on a scrapbook page, or it will overpower the photographs.

Hints: Cover the entire area with thick, dark crayon. You cannot engrave into the acrylic paint if there is no crayon underneath.

• Oil pastels are easier to use because they produce a thicker covering.

• Let the paint dry overnight so that it does not flake.

Technique Tools & Materials

Acrylic paint, black or dark color
Crayons or bright-colored oil pastels
Medium paintbrush
Toothpick
White card stock

Instructions

1. Cover entire design surface with crayons, alternating colors about every square inch.

2. Paint over the entire design with acrylic paint and allow to dry completely.

3. Etch design details into the paint, using a toothpick. This will reveal crayon color underneath paint.

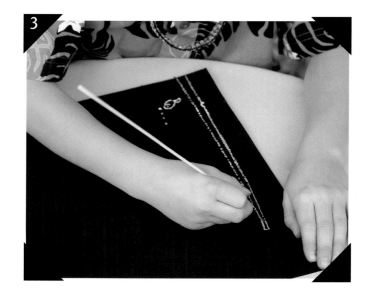

P R O J E C T

I LOVE TURKEY

Project Tools & Materials

Fall-colored pencils

Leaf, natural or die-cut

Photograph

Scissors

Instructions

1. Follow instructions for making **Crayon Etching** on page 94.

2. Place a leaf on crayon-etching paper. Using a toothpick, etch around the leaf.

3. Remove the leaf and begin etching the veins of the leaf. Make several leaves.

4. Cut around each leaf and set aside.

5. Crop and border the photograph and glue onto the card stock.

6. Glue the leaves onto the layout page, slightly overlapping the photograph. If they run off the page, cut away excess.

7. Using colored pencils, narrate the page.

Things I Like To Do

• To make this page showcasing the things you like to do, follow the instructions for **Crayon Etching** on page 94, using dark blue acrylic paint.

• Make certain that you etch a border around the blue paint to frame your picture.

My Art

• To make this page showcasing your best art work, follow the instructions for **Crayon Etching** on page 94, using purple acrylic paint.

• Try using the etched paper to border your photographs and cut out your narration.

P R O J E C T

Saddie, Con & Quaide

• Follow the instructions for **Crayon Etching** on page 94. On this page the narration and date are also etched into the crayon. Everything is cut from the etched paper and glued onto the background.

• Make your page more interesting by adding outside scenery around a picture taken outside.

PROJECT

LAKE POWELL

• Here is an example of crayon etchings being used to draw an underwater scene.

• Make the **Crayon Etching** paper following the instructions on page 94 and carve the underwater scene into the paper. Cut out strips of the scene and place them onto the sides of your photographs.

Wallpaper Collage

Ages 8 and up

Technique Tools & Materials

Colored paper
Glue stick
Pencil
Photographs
Scissors
Wallpaper

Instructions

1. On the back side of wallpaper, sketch images with a pencil. Cut out images and border them, using colored paper.

2. Using a glue stick, attach photographs and images onto a scrapbook page.

PROJECT

Harley Dude

Project Tools & Materials

Alphabet stickers
Black card stock
Brown scrap paper
Photo tape

Instructions

1. Follow instructions for making **Wallpaper Collage** above and sketch a tree, road, and clouds.

Hints: Most home improvement stores are willing to give out free samples of wallpaper.

• When selecting the wallpaper samples, take the time to select different colors, shades, textures, and patterns that complement each other. Patterns that go together nicely are stripes, florals, and prints. This is a great way to add interest, variety, and feel to a layout page.

2. Border images and photographs with black card stock.

3. Glue the clouds onto tan card stock. Glue the tree onto the layout page so it just overlaps one photograph.

4. Narrate, using alphabet stickers.

PROJECT

Doves

• Follow the instructions for making **Wallpaper Collage** on page 100 to make the doves on this page.

Hint: Clip art from your computer makes a great pattern for the doves.

PHOTOGRAPH WRAPS

PROJECT TOOLS & MATERIALS

Book bone

Card stocks (2)

Large needle

Pencil

Photo corners

Same-sized photographs (5)

Twine

INSTRUCTIONS

1. Cut the first wallpaper sample into a 10" square. Glue it into the center of a piece of card stock.

2. Cut the second piece of wallpaper into an 8" square. Measure to find the center of the square. Pierce two large holes through the wallpaper with a needle. Thread the twine through the holes so both ends of the twine are on the top of the wallpaper.

3. Glue the second piece of wallpaper in the center of the first piece.

4. To make the photograph wrap, cut another piece of card stock to measure 16" x 5". You may need to alter the dimensions depending on the size of your photographs.

5. Using a pencil, make a mark every 4" across the top and bottom of the paper.

6. Using the book bone and a ruler, score along 4" marks vertically. Fold along the creases accordion style.

7. Attach the first photograph onto the cover of the folded paper, using photo corners. Open the photograph collage paper and place photographs onto each inside page. Use the photo corners to hold the photographs into place.

8. Glue the photograph collage into the center of the twine.

9. Tie the twine around the collage.

PROJECT

SPRING FISHING

- Crazy wallpaper designs make this wallpaper collage interesting.

- Simply follow the **Wallpaper Collage** instructions on page 100 and make images resembling fish and plant life. The fish can overlap the photographs if you want.

- Remember, most fish are different colors so have fun creating a colorful underwater scene.

P R O J E C T
Las Vegas

- To make the waves and waterdrops, follow the instructions for making the **Wallpaper Collage** on page 100.

- This page would also work well for a scrapbook page about a day at the beach.

Motion Pictures

TECHNIQUE

This technique is similar to the way motion pictures were made in the early 1900s, before computers were invented to create cartoons.

Hint: Most cameras will not allow you to take photographs second by second, but even with small gaps in time you can capture a sequence of events.

Technique Tools & Materials

Camera with film
Glue stick
Ribbon, twine, yarn, or brads
Scissors
Scrap paper

Instructions

1. Identify an activity and begin snapping pictures one after the other. Have 4" x 6" photographs developed.

2. Cut 6" x 8" scrap pieces from paper. Glue photographs onto paper in the same location on each page. You will want the order of the photographs to have the first action photograph on the bottom and the final action photograph on the top.

3. On the top photograph, leave 1" bottom border. In sequence, cut off ¼" of each successive photograph border.

4. Line up top borders and tie together on the layout page with ribbon, twine, yarn, or brads.

PROJECT

TOO TIRED TO EAT

PROJECT TOOLS & MATERIALS

Acrylic paint
Card stock
Large needle
Paintbrush

Photographs
Ribbon
Squeegee

INSTRUCTIONS

1. Follow the instructions for **Motion Pictures** on page 106. If you want a patterned page, follow the instructions for **Acrylic Layers** on page 48. The page shown here used circular brush strokes.

2. To bind the photographs together on the layout page, line up the top edge of all the photographs. Thread the needle with ribbon. Page by page, run the ribbon through the top-left corner of each photograph page, then the patterned layout page. Remove the needle and tie a knot at the end of the ribbon.

3. Thread the ribbon through the right side of each photograph page, then the layout page. Tie the end into a knot. Make certain the knot pulls the ribbon tight across the photograph pages.

4. Glue the pattern page onto the card stock. You may need to crop the pattern paper to create the border. Using the squeegee, rub firmly across entire page.

5. Narrate the layout page, using a piece of scrap paper, a paintbrush, and the acrylic paint.

6. Once the paint has dried, cut around the words and glue them onto the layout page.

PROJECT
RUN TO ME

• On this page, the photographs and the pages have rounded edges. To make this page, follow the instructions for **Motion Pictures** on page 106. The petals on the flower are made by following the instructions for **Shaving Cream & Paint Paper** on page 12.

• Try using black-and-white photography for this project.

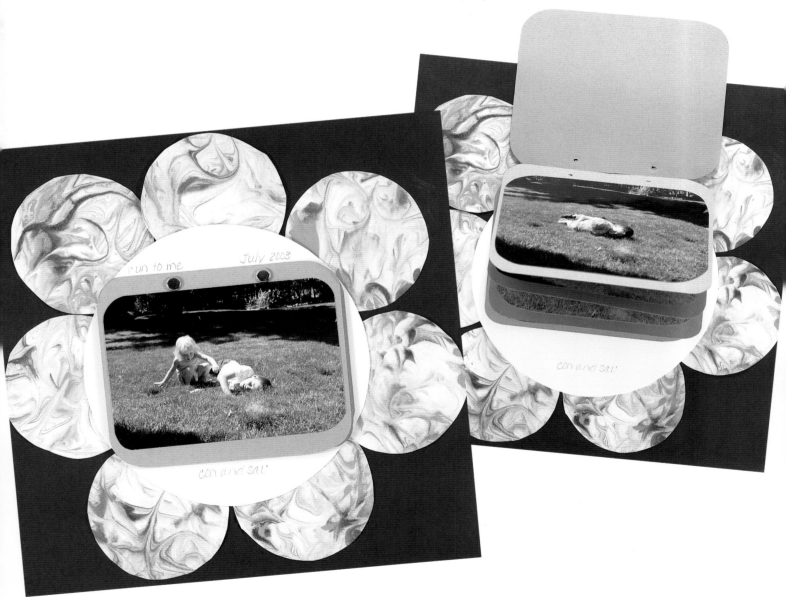

P R O J E C T

Watch Me Grow

• Make this page, following the instructions for making **Motion Pictures** on page 106 and using photographs from each year of your life. On this page, a line is drawn on the top of the page. The age is on the top and the year is at the bottom.

• This project is great for using up all those extra school photographs.

Swinging

- Follow instructions for **Motion Pictures** on page 106. Use ribbon to attach photographs onto the page.

- Try making a page with another activity such as running across a field or jumping rope.

P R O J E C T
SPRING SNOW

• To make this page, follow the instructions for **Motion Pictures** on page 106. Thread a piece of yarn through each side of your photograph book.

Hint: Trace around a glass to make snowballs.

Spray Paint

TECHNIQUE

Safety Note: Never spray paint inside of the house. Adults will need to supervise this activity.

Hints: When doing this technique, place a couple of objects at a time onto the paper. Overlapping different objects will create a beautiful silhouette effect.

• Use only white paper. Colored paper will change the colors of spray paint.

Technique Tools & Materials

Objects
Spray paints (3 colors)
Old towel or tarp
White card stock or watercolor paper

Instructions

1. Set up a spray area outside. Lay an old towel or tarp on ground. Make certain you are not close to anything that over-spray can damage.

2. Place paper or card stock onto towel and place two or three objects onto paper.

3. Spray a thin layer of the first color over objects. Hold can about 12" from paper while spraying.

4. Remove objects and replace with new ones. Select another color and spray.

5. Continue the spraying process until desired look is achieved. Allow paint to dry thoroughly in a well-ventilated area.

PROJECT
No More Flowers

Project Tools & Materials

Alphabet stickers

Glue stick

Leaves

Photograph

Spray paints: dark green, light green, red, yellow

Yellow card stock or scrap paper

Instructions

1. Follow the instructions for **Spray Paint** on page 112. Begin by using the red spray paint followed by the yellow, light green, and finish with the dark green.

Hint: You can use the same leaves over and again. Just be careful not to smear the paint onto your paper.

2. Let the paint dry completely. Crop and border the photograph with yellow paper.

3. Once the paper has dried, glue the photograph onto the page. Narrate, using alphabet stickers.

The Lemonade Stand

- For this project, use two pages and make scrapbook pages here and on 115 at same time.

- This project would be a great idea for showcasing your schoolwork.

- Follow instructions for **Spray Paint** on page 112, using die-cuts as your objects.

The Lemonade Stand

There was a nice lady who had
a plan.

The kids in the neighborhood
would make up her clan.

We will save the animals in this
land.

To do it, let's make a Lemonade
Stand.

We'll sell drinks, candy,
necklaces, and much more.

And soon customers will be
knocking at our door.

The Animal Sanctuary will get
the money we make.

Because, don't all animals
deserve a break?

Summer 1999

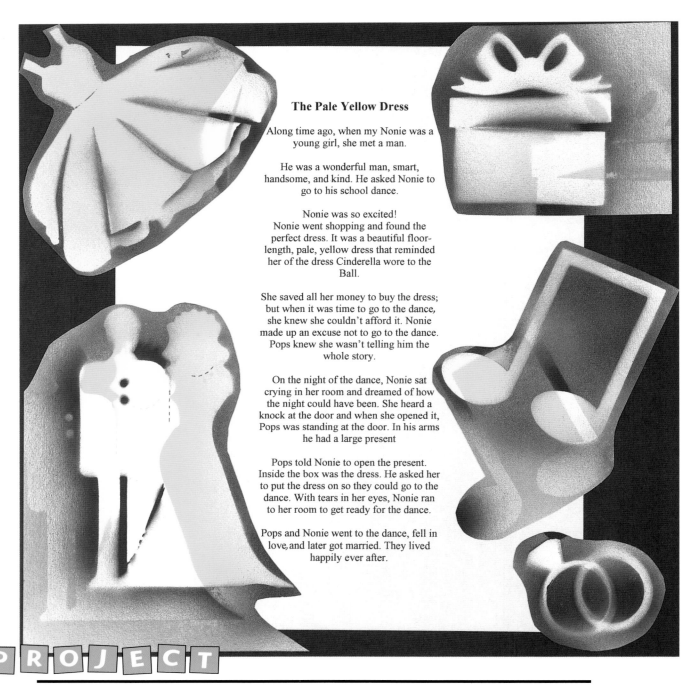

The Pale Yellow Dress

Along time ago, when my Nonie was a young girl, she met a man.

He was a wonderful man, smart, handsome, and kind. He asked Nonie to go to his school dance.

Nonie was so excited! Nonie went shopping and found the perfect dress. It was a beautiful floor-length, pale, yellow dress that reminded her of the dress Cinderella wore to the Ball.

She saved all her money to buy the dress; but when it was time to go to the dance, she knew she couldn't afford it. Nonie made up an excuse not to go to the dance. Pops knew she wasn't telling him the whole story.

On the night of the dance, Nonie sat crying in her room and dreamed of how the night could have been. She heard a knock at the door and when she opened it, Pops was standing at the door. In his arms he had a large present

Pops told Nonie to open the present. Inside the box was the dress. He asked her to put the dress on so they could go to the dance. With tears in her eyes, Nonie ran to her room to get ready for the dance.

Pops and Nonie went to the dance, fell in love, and later got married. They lived happily ever after.

PROJECT

Let Me Tell You a Story About Someone Special

• Capture something special. Ask your parents or grandparents to tell you a story about their past. Write or type the story and glue it onto the first page.

• For this project, use two pages and spray-paint die-cuts for the scrapook pages here and on page 117.

- Crop and border a picture of the person who told you the story, or the person the story is about.

- This page would make a great keepsake or gift for a special person.

Photograph Fun

TECHNIQUE

This section gives some ideas on how you can make your photographs and scrapbook pages fun.

Just remember, you need to have a good sense of humor to make the projects. Learn to laugh at yourself and have fun. Be crazy, creative, and use your imagination. You and your friends will have a blast.

Hint: Always begin by making the images larger than you expect they will need to be. You can always cut portions of the photograph away; but you can not add to the picture.

Technique Tools & Materials

Background paper
Card stocks, assorted colors
Colored pens
Colored pencils
Glue
Paper scraps, assorted colors
Photographs
Ribbon
Scissors

Instructions

1. Border a photograph with card stock and glue it onto a patterned background page.

2. Sketch images such as hats, hairdos, outfits, quotes, and dream bubbles onto various colors of card stock.

3. Cut out the images. You may need to make adjustments so they fit your photograph properly.

4. Place the images sporadically around the layout page.

5. Glue ribbons, or other decorations to the page.

6. Repeat with another photograph.

PROJECT

WHO SHOULD I BE TODAY?

PROJECT TOOLS & MATERIALS

Clear plastic report cover

INSTRUCTIONS

1. Follow the instructions for **Photograph Fun** on page 118. Border your photograph with card stock and glue it onto the inside of the plastic report cover.

2. Sketch hats, hairdos, beards, mustaches, and outfits onto various colors of card stock.

3. Cut out the images. You may need to make adjustments so they fit your photograph properly.

4. Tape each image onto the clear plastic report cover.

5. The images should make the photograph look really goofy, but when the plastic cover is turned, the photograph will be nice and perfect.

PROJECT

What Were They Really Thinking?

• Have you ever wondered what people were really thinking when posing for a photograph? This page gives you some funny ideas. Follow the instructions for making **Photograph Fun** on page 118.

• To make your own quote bubbles, use clipart from your computer and type in funny thoughts. Or you can draw your own and attach them onto the photograph.

PROJECT

Talents

- To make this page, follow the instructions for the **Who Should I Be Today** project on page 119.

- Glue a class photograph onto the inside of the report cover and attach clip art onto the outside showing the talents of the others in your class.

Twisted Ribbon

TECHNIQUE

Ages 7 and up

Hints: Have a wet rag or paper towels handy. Your fingers can get a little gooey.

• Since you are making images using ribbon, they will tend to be somewhat abstract.

 ## Word to Know

Abstract means freely developing form and design or a nontraditional look or feel. This will enhance your layout page and make it interesting and beautiful.

Technique Tools & Materials
- Card stock
- Clear adhesive-backed bumpers
- Glue stick
- Thin ribbon

Instructions

1. Cut your ribbon into pieces, the size will depend on the image you are creating.

2. Lay one piece of ribbon onto a piece of card stock.

3. Apply glue onto ¼" of each end.

4. Press one end onto the layout page, then twist or turn ribbon and press the other end onto the page.

5. Place bumpers on each of the corners. This will keep the ribbon from smashing when placed inside a book.

P R O J E C T

May Rain

Project Tools & Materials

Green patterned scrap paper
Photographs
Pink alphabet stickers
Pink card stock
Ribbons: green, pink, white

Instructions

1. Crop and border each photograph and glue onto a piece of pink card stock.

2. To make the grass, place photo tape onto one end of the green ribbon. On a slight angle, press the end of the ribbon on the bottom-left corner of the layout page.

3. Continue the process, weaving the ribbon up and down along the bottom of the page.

4. To make the raindrops, cut several pieces of the white ribbon approximately 7" long. Follow the instructions for **Twisted Ribbon** on page 122.

5. To make the border, place glue on the end of the pink ribbon. Press the ribbon onto one edge of the layout page. Run the ribbon across the edge until you meet a raindrop. Cut the ribbon on an angle and glue into place on the page.

6. Continue the same process until the entire layout page has a border.

7. Narrate the page using alphabet stickers.

FALL 2002

LEAVES EVERYWHERE

• Follow the instructions for **Twisted Ribbon** on page 122. To make the leaves on this page, sketch leaves onto the layout page and then glue one end of your ribbon onto the page. Twist the ribbon into the leaf shape, adding a dot of glue every so often to attach the leaf onto the sketch.

Morning Sun

• Place a couple of photograph stickers close together in a small square shape on the layout page. Follow instructions for **Twisted Ribbon** on page 122. Attach the bow into the center of three photo stickers and glue a button into the center of the flower.

July 2003

Metric Equivalency Chart

mm–millimeters   cm–centimeters
inches to millimeters and centimeters

inches	mm	cm		inches	mm	cm		inches	mm	cm
⅛	3	0.3		1¼	32	3.2		5	127	12.7
¼	6	0.6		1½	38	3.8		6	152	15.2
⅜	10	1.0		1¾	44	4.4		7	178	17.8
½	13	1.3		2	51	5.1		8	203	20.3
⅝	16	1.6		2½	64	6.4		9	229	22.9
¾	19	1.9		3	76	7.6		10	254	25.4
⅞	22	2.2		3½	89	8.9		11	279	27.9
1	25	2.5		4	102	10.2		12	305	30.5

Index

About the Author

Nikki Larsen's enthusiasm for developing *Scribbles, Stickers & Glue: A Kids' Guide to Scrapbooking* evolved out of her passion for creating fun craft projects for her children. She believes much can be gained from the process of creating an art project which in turn brings satisfaction when viewing the end result. Working with her children, Conner and Savannah, Nikki observed that arts-and-crafts projects offer an exciting avenue for learning.

Nikki's attraction for being an artist and author is rooted in her upbringing. She spent countless hours painting watercolors with her mother, who was an accomplished freelance writer, photographer, and artist. Her father, a local business owner and entrepreneur, was always her most constructive critic. He taught Nikki the importance of persistence and the value of always doing your best work.

Apple~Eye L.C.—the company Nikki and her husband have created, operates on a simple, but sound principle: develop products that make a difference. The company's theme is tied directly to the dedication she holds toward raising her children.

Acknowledgments

I want to give my sincere thanks and appreciation to my family, friends, and the Binford Street neighborhood children. Your support, help, and advice has been of more value to me than you will ever know. A special thanks to Jim and Frankie Larsen, your love and guidance in my life has made a tremendous difference. Becky, my "in-house" editor and moral support lifeline, thank you! Thanks Jo Packham, your faith in me has been an inspiration through the process of writing this book.

To Conner and Savannah—you have been my most valuable instructors—I love you. And to my husband—the greatest gift of all. Thanks Mom and Dad—I know you are watching.